FROGS

above: Red-eyed tree frog, *Agalychnis callidryas* (Mexico and Central America).
opposite: Tree frog, *Hyla marmorata* (Peru).
previous page: Pacific tree frog, *Hyla regilla* (Washington).

With thanks to Gregory A. Green, Ron Crombie, and Roy McDiarmid of the National Museum of Natural History, Smithsonian Institution, and Gary Stolz of the U.S. Fish and Wildlife Service.

All photos © Art Wolfe except: pg. 7 top and pg. 9 © Gavriel Jecan/Art Wolfe, Inc.; pg. 14 © C. W. Myers/American Museum of Natural History; pg. 16 © William E. Duellman/University of Kansas Natural History Museum; pg. 20 © Doug Cheeseman/Peter Arnold, Inc.; pg. 23 © John Netherton; pg. 24 © R. Andrew Odum/Peter Arnold, Inc.; pg. 25 © Matt Meadows/Peter Arnold, Inc.; pg. 27 © Hans Pfletschinger/Peter Arnold, Inc.; pg. 28 © Kevin Schafer/Peter Arnold, Inc.

Published by Crown Publishers, Inc., a Random House company,
201 East 50th Street, New York, New York 10022
CROWN is a trademark of Crown Publishers, Inc.
Printed in Hong Kong
http://www.randomhouse.com/

*Library of Congress Cataloging-in-Publication Data*
Martin, James, 1950– . Frogs / by James Martin; photographs by Art Wolfe.—1st ed.
p. cm.
Includes index. Summary: Describes the physical characteristics and behavior patterns of different kinds of frogs.
ISBN 0-517-70905-8 (trade). — ISBN 0-517-70906-6 (lib. bdg.) 1. Frogs—Juvenile literature.
[1. Frogs.] I. Wolfe, Art, ill. II. Title. QL668.E2M32 1997 597.8'9–dc21 96-29879

10 9 8 7 6 5 4 3 2 1 First Edition

# FROGS

by JAMES MARTIN

photographs by
ART WOLFE

Crown Publishers, Inc.
New York

In the dark, damp forests of Argentina lives a warty green lump. Despite its bright colors, this horned frog is hard to see against the mosses and fallen leaves. Just by staying very still, this frog is hunting. The fleshy "horns" above the frog's eyes break up its outline, camouflaging its presence. Animals often fail to recognize irregular shapes. When an insect or small rodent strays too close, the frog leaps forward and grabs it in its mouth. It has such a huge appetite, it may even try to eat its own brothers and sisters. This fat frog is like a stomach with legs. But even the tubby horned frog looks small in comparison to the world's largest frog: the Goliath frog of Africa, which grows to the size of a flattened soccer ball. The smallest frog is a tiny Cuban species barely the size of a pencil eraser. In between these two extremes are 2,700 other kinds of frogs, which come in an amazing variety of shapes and sizes and colors.

Ornate horned frog, *Ceratophrys ornata* (Argentina).

ithin this variety, all frogs share some common traits. All have triangular bodies and large mouths. Their heads join their bodies without a neck in between. Their front legs are short and thin, but their rear legs are thick and powerful. Instead of walking or running, frogs hop and leap. In the middle of a long jump, they look like Superman flying.

Frogs have long toes and often have webbed feet for swimming. Their rear feet act like a diver's swim fins. Tree frogs and other climbers possess suckers on the tips of their toes. The suckers stick to slick surfaces, such as wet leaves, so the frogs can climb.

Two frogs even fly with their feet. Wallace's gliding frog and the Malay gliding frog can sail up to 50 feet from one tree to another. They suck in their stomachs to form a hollowed-out surface, then they leap. The webbing between their toes fills with air like a parachute and holds them aloft. Extra-wide sucker disks at the end of their toes catch air, too.

Webbed foot of bullfrog, *Rana catesbeiana* (United States).

above: Red-eyed tree frog, *Agalychnis callidryas* (Mexico and Central America).
opposite: Poison dart frog, *Epipedobates trivittatus* (Peru).

Tree frog, *Hyla geographica* (Peru).

Frogs are amphibians. So are newts and salamanders. Amphibians bridge the gap between fish and reptiles. Fish live only in water and absorb oxygen from the water with their gills, while reptiles live on land and breathe air with their lungs. But an amphibian starts its life as a water creature and then transforms into a land animal as it matures.

When amphibians hatch, they breathe with gills and through their skin. They often swim with fins like fish. As they grow up, they lose their gills and develop lungs—a process called metamorphosis. At the same time, their fins disappear and legs take their place. As adults, frogs breathe with their lungs and through their skin and through membranes in their mouths.

Most amphibians are members of the Anura, the order of frogs and toads. Frogs tend to have thin, wet, smooth skin, while toads have thick, dry, warty skin. Frogs tend to have webbed feet, while toads don't. However, there are froggy toads and toady frogs. The boundary between the two is unclear, and even scientists don't worry too much about the distinction.

The first amphibians evolved from fishes about 350 million years ago. At that time, only plants, insects, and other creatures without backbones lived on the land. Amphibians were the first animals with backbones to live out of water. The oldest frog fossil dates back 190 million years. All animals with backbones living on land today, including birds, snakes, and mammals—and yes, even people!—have amphibian ancestors.

Western toad, *Bufo boreas* (Southern Alaska to Northern California, Montana, and Colorado).

Frogs are survivors. They have lived through numerous disasters in the earth's history. The conditions that killed the dinosaurs spared frogs. These cold-blooded creatures survived by adapting to changing conditions on the planet.

Cold-blooded animals use heat from the sun and the air to keep warm and to help digest their food. When the temperature drops, warm-blooded animals need to find ways to keep warm, while cold-blooded animals simply become less active. Cold-blooded creatures also need less food. Warm-blooded animals stay warm by extracting calories from food. A warm-blooded animal needs ten times as much food as a cold-blooded animal of the same size. When food is scarce, frogs and other cold-blooded critters can survive longer than mammals and other warm-blooded animals.

Frogs thrive in warm, wet climates. However, hardy frogs inhabit some of the planet's driest and coldest spots, exploiting brief opportunities to feed and breed. Depending on the environmental conditions, frogs may hibernate, bury themselves, change color, produce poisons, freeze solid, or display other astonishing behaviors. The story of frogs is a tale of almost magical adaptations.

left: Toad, *Bufo typhonius* complex (Peru).
above: Green tree frog, *Phyllomedusa bicolor* (Brazil).
opposite: Grasping frog, *Phyllomedusa vaillanti* (Peru).

A frog's skin is often the key to its survival. The most important feature of frog skin is common to all amphibians: when underwater, they breathe through it. Their skin absorbs oxygen directly from the water itself.

Instead of scales, feathers, or fur, slime covers their skin. The slime prevents them from drying out. Contrary to popular myth, touching a frog will not bring on warts. Compounds in their skin actually act to prevent disease. In fact, drug companies are developing treatments based on frog-created chemicals to fight disease in people.

White's tree frog, *Litoria caerulea* (New Guinea and Australia).

Tomato frog, *Discophus antongilli* (Madagascar).

One African frog's skin changes with the temperature. In the heat of the day, its skin turns from dark green to white, which reflects heat the way a mirror reflects light. Beads of moisture sweat from special pores. As the sweat evaporates, the frog cools. Without these adaptations, the frog would die.

The skin of the tomato frog of Madagascar, which looks a bit like a tomato dropped from a great height, protects in another way. When a snake approaches, the frog puffs itself up like a balloon. Sometimes the snake decides the frog is too big to swallow, but if the snake still tries to eat it, the tomato frog secretes a white, gluelike liquid from its skin. The liquid tastes bad and sticks to the snake like gum. The snake slithers away, and now knows to avoid tomato-colored frogs.

Poison dart frog, *Dendrobates histrionicus* (Colombia and Ecuador).

In the jungles of Colombia, the Embera Choco natives hunt the world's most poisonous land animal: *Phyllobates terribilis,* the golden poison frog. Its skin glistens with deadly poison, and its touch can kill. A single frog contains enough poison to kill eight people.

Frog poison is specialized slime. Natives rub the tips of their darts against the golden poison frog's skin. They take care not to touch the frog with their fingers, using a leaf as a glove. After bringing down an animal with a poison dart, they must cut out the contaminated meat to avoid poisoning themselves.

There are approximately 170 kinds of poison dart frogs, all of which live in the jungles of Central and South America. The largest grow to three inches, while the smallest reach only one-half inch. Poison dart frogs advertise their toxicity with warning colors that signify danger. Ice blues, blazing reds, dandelion yellows, and neon greens advise potential attackers to beware.

above: Poison dart frog, *Dendrobates leucomelas* (Venezuela).
right: Poison dart frog, *Dendrobates azureus* (Surinam).
opposite: Golden poison frog, *Phyllobates terribilis* (Colombia).

15

Most frogs depend on camouflage, not poison, to keep them safe. If you can't be seen, you can't be eaten. Most camouflage is simple. Green frogs live on green leaves, while brown toads live on dead leaves or dirt.

For some frogs, color is just a starting point. The casque-headed frog, like the horned frog, has developed an unfroglike profile. Pyramids top its eyes. Jagged edges poke from its body. Any predator looking for the smooth, bulbous shape of a frog might not notice the broken outline of the casque-headed frog.

Twin spots on the backs of some frogs and toads look like eyes. These "false eyes" give the impression that the entire animal is a large head with unblinking eyes watching out for predators sneaking up behind it.

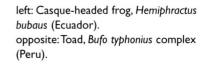

left: Casque-headed frog, *Hemiphractus bubaus* (Ecuador).
opposite: Toad, *Bufo typhonius* complex (Peru).

Many frogs imitate unappetizing things. This is called mimicry. Solomon Island leaf frogs have adopted the shape and color of fallen leaves. Only the sharpest eyes can pick them out of the leaf litter on the forest floor.

In Central and South America, some non-poisonous frogs have evolved the colors of poison dart frogs. Predators mistake the harmless frogs for their poisonous relatives and steer clear.

Others avoid notice by looking unappealing. The skin of a Tambopata River frog in Peru resembles bird droppings on a leaf—a characteristic that tends to kill the appetite of even the most famished predator.

Solomon Island leaf frogs, *Ceratobatrachus quentheri* (Solomon Islands).

Frogs have adapted to life in desert areas by finding unusual ways to conserve water.

Most frogs burrow underground to avoid drying out. The skin of the white-spotted burrowing frogs of Australia secretes a liquid that hardens and seals moisture inside. The frogs keep a reservoir of water in their bladder that can account for half their weight. They can also convert their fat to water, if necessary. The Aborigines use these frogs to quench their thirst. They dig up a frog, hold it to their mouth, and suck the water out of its bladder. This can be a life-saver for the Aborigines, but doesn't do much for the frog's chances.

The frogs sleep underground for up to seven years, waiting for the downpours they need in order to reproduce. When the rains arrive, the moisture soaks down into the earth and softens their skin. Like kissed princesses, the frogs awaken. They shed their skins and eat them for their first meal. Then they dig their way to the surface and head for the nearest puddle. There they will absorb a new supply of water to sustain them during the next drought. Quickly the frogs mate, then tunnel underground to await the next great rain.

In the Namib Desert, generations of African burrowing frogs live without ever feeling a raindrop. They spend their days buried in the sand, hiding from the blistering sun and drying winds. Each night they emerge to hunt. When morning comes, a fog forms. Dewdrops drip from desert plants and condense on the frogs themselves. The frogs lick up the dewdrops and absorb water through their skin. When laying eggs, these frogs must create their own pool in the sand. The mother frog covers her fertile eggs with a wet coating of infertile eggs.

White-spotted burrowing frog, *Heleioporus albopunctatus* (Australia).

Frogs have also adapted to life in many of the coldest corners of the earth. Frogs usually survive in cold climates by hiding from freezing weather. They spend the winter hibernating at the bottom of deep lakes, where the water never freezes.

Wood frogs, however, survive the winter cold by *allowing* themselves to freeze. As the temperature dips, the moisture on the frog's skin turns to ice, and soon the frog is frozen solid. When spring comes, the frogsicle defrosts and shivers back to life. This should be impossible. Water expands when it freezes. When other animals freeze, the expanding ice breaks their cell walls. But amazingly, this frog's cells contain a natural antifreeze that keeps them intact.

The cold waters of Lake Titicaca harbor a unique species of frog. Situated at 12,500 feet above sea level in the Andes between Bolivia and Peru, the water, like the air, contains less oxygen than at lower elevations. To capture more oxygen from the water, the Lake Titicaca frog grows extra flaps of skin. Just as a larger sail catches more of a breeze than a smaller sail, the extra skin gives the frog more surface area, so it comes in contact with more water and therefore more oxygen. Even so, the frog soon uses up all the oxygen around it. In response, the frog does "push-ups." Its flapping skin churns the water, cycling fresh oxygen its way.

Wood frog, *Rana sylvatica* (Canada and northeastern United States).

Barking tree frog, *Hyla gratiosa* (North Carolina, Florida, and Louisiana).

Frogs are the birds of the cold-blooded world. Snakes hiss and some geckos bark, but no other group of reptiles or amphibians makes music the way frogs do. During the breeding season, frogs twitter, chirp, trumpet, click, and ribbit each night. Generally, male frogs do the serenading to let female frogs know they are available for mating. Females remain mum while choosing.

A frog doesn't open its mouth and bellow like an opera singer. Instead, it compresses its lungs while keeping its mouth and nostrils shut. This forces air across the vocal cords and into a pouch below the mouth that fills with vibrating air and radiates sound to the outside like the skin of a bass drum.

Frogs compete for air time. With individual frogs of many species calling at the same time, the night can sound like a radio tuned to every station at once. Frogs share the night by reserving certain frequencies and times to themselves. Each species uses its own set of frequencies, and females of each species hear the sounds made by their males especially well. No two males call at the same time, but as soon as one frog stops calling, another starts his song. They can detect windows of silence in a fraction of a second.

The female Malaysian tree frog takes matters into her own hands. When she hears males calling, she climbs onto a dense bed of reeds and taps her feet. The males pick up the vibrations and head toward her.

Gray tree frog, *Hyla chrysoscelis*
(Eastern United States).

Frogs undergo an amazing metamorphosis. Like most amphibians, frogs begin life in the water. A female frog deposits her eggs in water. As she does so, the male grasps the female from behind and sprays the eggs with sperm, fertilizing them.

The eggs stick together in large jellied clumps or as ropes of goo with the eggs strung like pearls. Some frogs lay a single egg, while others deposit up to 35,000, but most produce only a few thousand eggs. In streams, the parents fasten the clump to a rock or root so the current doesn't sweep the eggs downstream. Their duty done, the parents leave for good.

Out of the eggs hatch a cloud of tiny tadpoles, but without parental care, only a few will live to grow into frogs. Tadpoles are like little fish. They have gills, fins, and a tail.

As the tadpoles grow and change, they become more froglike each day. They sprout legs and lose their fins. The torso absorbs the tail. And most amazingly, they develop lungs so that, when the process finishes, they can hop onto land and live as naturally as they did in water. Though when they first use their lungs, they can be seen gasping for air like drowning swimmers.

Most tadpoles change into frogs over the course of a few weeks, but in some species the change takes only days, while others remain tadpoles for a year or two.

Metamorphosis of the common European frog, *Rana temporaria* (World except New Zealand and desert regions).

Most frogs lay thousands of eggs and then leave, but some frogs lay only a few eggs and try to protect their offspring at least until they hatch and sometimes until they are full-grown.

The poison dart frog *Dendrobates pumilio* lays between two and sixteen eggs on the rain forest floor. She then stands guard over her clutch until they hatch. When the first tadpole emerges from its egg, it wiggles onto her back. With her tadpole clinging to her, she climbs to the top of the forest canopy. She looks for large leaves that hold puddles of water. When she finds a satisfactory pool, she drops off her tadpole and returns to the other eggs. She repeats the process for each tadpole, scattering her brood throughout the forest. A roving predator might find one tadpole, but it is unlikely to find all of them.

A couple of times each week, she returns to feed her young. This strategy pays off. A high percentage of the young survive long enough to reproduce.

The marsupial frog keeps its eggs in a pouch like a kangaroo. When the eggs hatch and the tadpoles are ready to set out on their own, the mother opens the pouch with her toes and pours them into the water. The males of some casque-headed frog species perform the same duty for their young.

Poison dart frog, *Dendrobates pumilio* (Costa Rica).

The history of frogs has been one of amazing adaptation, but today, all over the world, frogs and other amphibians are vanishing. Australian scientists discovered the gastric brooding frog, which raised its young in its mouth, in 1973. Now none exist.

The population of golden toads in Costa Rica crashed almost overnight. The red-legged tree frog can no longer be found in the forests of California and Oregon. These could be normal population swings or hibernation cycles unknown to science. However, most scientists have more pessimistic theories.

Scientists call environmentally sensitive creatures like frogs an "indicator species." When the population of these species declines, it may mean that the ecosystem is in trouble. The disappearance of certain frogs could be a sign that something is dangerously wrong on our planet. Perhaps the thinning of the ozone layer, which was triggered by man-made chemicals, creates conditions that hurt frogs. The decline of frogs may show that global warming is indeed a fact. Perhaps pollution poisons them. The loss of habitat from logging and farming prevents some frogs from moving to mating areas.

Mankind appears to be partly or completely responsible in every case. No matter which problems account for the decline, clearly frogs can't adapt. If we don't listen to the amphibians and take better care of our planet, the world may become uninhabitable for humans, too. We must listen to their warnings just as we listen to their songs.

Red-legged frog, *Rana aurora* (British Columbia to California).

JAMES MARTIN'S books for children have been lavished with praise, garnering honors from the American Library Association, the National Science Teachers Association, and the International Reading Association, among others. Previous titles include *Chameleons: Dragons in the Trees; Tentacles: The Amazing World of Octopus, Squid, and Their Relatives; Hiding Out: Camouflage in the Wild;* and *Living Fossils: Animals That Have Withstood the Test of Time.* Mr. Martin lives in Seattle, Washington.

ART WOLFE is one of the world's leading nature photographers. In his twenty-year career, he has photographed all manner of bird and beast, from bears to owls, penguins to wolves. His images appear regularly in many of the world's major magazines. He has published thirty-four books, including the award-winning *Migrations* and *Light on the Land* as well as *Bald Eagles: Their Life and Behavior in North America; Rainforests: Water, Fire, Earth and Air;* and *The Art of Photographing Nature.*

Tree frog, *Hyla calcarata* (Peru).

## INDEX